Now Playing: Learning Communication Through Film

Russell F. Proctor II
Sam Lapin

Northern Kentucky University

Assisted By:
Carl Allison
Jennifer Benjamin
Kathleen Blomer
Adam Diebold
Laura Eisenmenger
Kathleen Francis
Laura Linville
Valerie Macarie
John Renaker
Kathleen Renaker
Roseanna Rock
Leigh Ann Schroeder
Northern Kentucky University

And

T. J. Jenkins
James Madison University

D1733615

New York   Oxford
OXFORD UNIVERSITY PRESS
2006

INTRODUCTION

Communication is a human necessity—without it, we could scarcely coexist. Observing and analyzing communication patterns, interactions, and the many other intricacies of human contact is how we learn to project ourselves more effectively. Often times it is difficult to evaluate our own communication processes in an objective manner—but watching people communicating in films can be an excellent way to identify and understand many aspects of communication. Closely watching others engaged in communication on film can help bring theories and concepts to life.

This manual contains a section on **Feature Film Scenes**—a variety of specific scenes from a number of different films that illustrate the good, the bad, and the ugly of human interaction. A second section, **Full-Length Feature Films,** provides examples of entire films that provide insights into human communication, with a detailed synopsis of the movie along with discussion questions to prompt critical thinking.

Looking at the various characters in these films struggle with communication can be liberating as well as enlightening—we can observe it from a distance and, without being too self-conscious, pick up on both the good and the bad habits that can lead us to become better communicators. Have fun learning!

CONTENTS

Section II: Full-Length Feature Films   18

Section III: Feature Film Web Sites of Interest: 53

INDEX BY COMMUNICATION CONCEPTS

SECTION I
FEATURE FILM SCENES

Each of the entries in this section is a "stand alone" scene that illustrates communication concepts (with a strong focus on interpersonal communication). The scenes are listed below in alphabetical order; they are also arranged by category in the index at the beginning of the book. The time locations of the scenes are measured from the opening moment of the movie, just after the display of the film company (in other words, don't begin counting on your timer until all the previews on the video are finished).

Film: Almost Famous
Year: 2000
Central Concept: Self-Disclosure
Related Concepts: Identity Management, Group Communication
Approximate Scene Location: 96 minutes into the 122-minute movie
Approximate Scene Length: 4 minutes
Opening Line: Brief shot of plane flying through storm (no dialogue)
Closing Line: "Thank God we're all alive. We're going to make it!" (To capture facial expressions of the passengers after they realize they will survive, don't cut until scene ends, about 10 seconds after last line of dialogue)

Scene Description: A 1970s rock band is on tour when its plane is caught in a violent storm. The prospect of imminent death moves several members of the group and its entourage to reveal facts and feelings they had previously kept to themselves. Some of the self-disclosing messages are positive; others are upsetting and disruptive. The scene offers a good foundation for exploring several dimensions of self-revelation: Reasons for opening up, the conditions under which disclosure is likely to occur, and the risks and benefits of candor. (Note: the scene contains language that may offend some viewers)

Discussion Questions:
1. Place the self-disclosures offered in this scene on a continuum, ranging from "appropriate under most conditions" to "inappropriate under most conditions." Describe the conditions under which the disclosures might be appropriate/inappropriate.
2. Which members of the group have been engaging in high levels of identity management with the others? What will happen to the management of their identities now that they've made these revelations?
3. Describe the following group communication concepts at work in this scene: ripple effect, conformity, openness and boundaries.
4. Have you ever made a self-disclosure in a group of people that you later regretted? Discuss why you made the disclosure and how you managed your identity in later interactions with those people.

Film: American President, The
Year: 1996
Central Concept: Communication Competence
Related Concept: Perception
Approximate Scene Location: 25 minutes into the 114-minute film
Approximate Scene Length: 5 minutes
Opening Line: "Richard, it wasn't funny"
Closing Line: "Thanks for asking me"

Scene Description: Sydney Ellen Wade is an environmental lobbyist; Andrew Shepherd is the President of the United States. After an embarrassing meeting at the White House where Wade attempts to be assertive (only to find herself trying to leave through the wrong door), Shepherd calls to ask her for a date. Wade does not believe the

President would be phoning her, much less asking her out; thus she responds inappropriately and awkwardly to Shepherd's call.

Discussion Questions:
1. How are Wade's reactions during the phone call affected by her perceptual filters?
2. How would you rate Wade's communication competence in this scene? Shepherd's?
3. Discuss how this scene demonstrates the transactional nature of communication.
4. Discuss how the messages in this scene have both content and relationship dimensions.
5. Was it fair for Shepherd to do this to Wade? Why or why not?

Film: At First Sight
Year: 1998
Central Concepts: Perception, Nonverbal
Related Concept: Culture
Approximate Scene Location: 78 minutes into the 126-minute film
Approximate Scene Length: 5 minutes
Opening Line: "What's going on?"
Closing Line: "Take me home"

Scene Description: Virgil Adamson, who has been blind since he was three years old, undergoes extensive surgery to restore his eyesight. With his newly acquired vision, he has difficulty making sense of the world. As he develops his ability to define shapes and distance, Virgil becomes confused by new images. He finds that assigning meaning to sensory information and nonverbal behavior does not come naturally; it is a learned skill. For instance, he doesn't know how to interpret nonverbal relational cues, and thus becomes confused when he sees his girlfriend give her business partner a kiss. He asks for interpretations of her facial expressions by saying, "I don't understand what your face means." Virgil feels uncomfortable and tries to leave the party—but in doing so he walks into a large glass room divider, shattering the glass and cutting himself.

Discussion Questions:
1. Give examples of how Virgil selects, organizes, and interprets sensory information in this scene.
2. Discuss the common tendencies in perception that Virgil follows (or doesn't follow).
3. Identify the nonverbal cues that Virgil does and does not understand, and how he makes sense of them.
4. It could be argued that Virgil has entered another culture by entering the sighted world. Argue for or against that proposition, using concepts from your textbook.

Film: Before Sunrise
Year: 1994
Central Concept: Nonverbal
Related Concepts: Relational Stages, Emotions
Approximate Scene Location: 27 minutes into the 100-minute film
Approximate Scene Length: 2 minutes
Opening Line: "This is pretty neat" (regarding the record store)
Closing Line: None (the scene is all nonverbal once they get in the listening booth)

Scene Description: Jesse and Celine meet on a train ride from Budapest to Paris. They take an immediate liking to each other and decide, on a whim, to spend a day/night together in Vienna before Jesse boards a plane home to the United States (Celene is French and is returning to Paris). During their evening in Vienna, they stop in a record store. Celine is interested in an album and Jesse suggests they go into the listening booth to see if she likes it. They enter the cramped booth together and the music plays. They are clearly falling for each other, but they are still early in their relationship. Their nonverbal cat-and-mouse games in the listening booth, which last more than a minute, illustrate well the interaction between eye contact, proxemics, and relational stages.

Discussion Questions:
1. Describe the effect of proxemics on the eye contact between Jesse and Celine. What rules for eye contact are being followed?
2. How do you think these two feel about each other? What stage of relationship do you think they are in? What nonverbal cues lead you to your conclusions?
3. How do you feel watching these two in the booth? Identify three different emotions.

Film: Clueless
Year: 1995
Central Concept: Language
Related Concepts: Culture, Communication Competence
Approximate Scene Location: 30 seconds into the 97-minute film
Approximate Scene Length: 4 minutes
Opening Line: "Did I show you the lumped-out jeep daddy got me?"
Closing Line: "If she doesn't do the assignment, I can't do mine"

Scene Description: Cher and her friends live in their own "contempo-casual" culture and speak their own language (depicted throughout this scene with words such as "jeepin," "outie," and "buggin'"). Their linguistic code gives them a sense of shared identity and excludes those who are not in their group. Near the end of the scene, Cher uses her group's jargon in a public speaking context and her speech is not successful, demonstrating that language which is appropriate for an informal context is not appropriate for a formal one. This scene could be particularly useful for hybrid courses in which interpersonal, intercultural, and public speaking competence is addressed.

Discussion Questions:
1. Identify words/terms used by Cher and her friends that are unique to their culture. Which words/terms were not familiar to you?
2. Why do teenagers create new words and/or give old words new meanings?
3. Is it appropriate to use slang and jargon in public speeches?
4. Discuss this scene in terms of interpersonal, intercultural, and public speaking competence.

Film: Dead Man Walking
Year: 1996
Central Concept: Perception (Stereotyping and Prejudice)
Related Concepts: Communication Climate, Listening, Language
Approximate Scene Location: 40 minutes into the 120-minute film
Approximate Scene Length: 3 minutes
Opening Line: "Rain, rain, rain . . . that's a bad sign" (in the middle of a prison cell discussion)
Closing Line: "Can we talk about something else?"

Scene Description: This scene is an interpersonal communication tour de force. Helen Prejean is a nun who befriends death-row prisoner Matthew Poncelet prior to his execution. She confronts Poncelet about his prejudices regarding African-Americans. Poncelet's perceptions and language are filled with stereotypes and generalizations about "niggers" and "coloreds." Prejean's questions and responses require him to think (which he doesn't seem to want to do) about inaccuracies in his generalizations. Some of her comments are loaded and get defensive reactions; most are reflective and allow Poncelet to hear his prejudices in another voice. When Prejean's probing digs too deep (she gets him to realize "it's lazy people you don't like," not blacks), Poncelet asks Prejean to change the subject—which she agrees to do. This scene is worthy of line-by-line analysis.

Discussion Questions:
1. What factors influenced Poncelet's perceptions, prejudices, and stereotypes?
2. What listening skills does Prejean use to draw information from Poncelet? How do these skills get/keep Poncelet talking and thinking?
3. What questions/statements by Prejean prompt a defensive response from Poncelet?
4. Discuss the use of responsible and irresponsible language in the scene and its relationship to communication   climate.

Film: Doctor, The
Year: 1991
Central Concept: Perception (Empathy and Roles)
Approximate Scene Location: 114 minutes into the 123-minute film
Approximate Scene Length: 3 minutes
Opening Line: "Any messages for me?"
Closing Line: "So, good luck. See you on my rounds"

Scene Description: Dr. Jack McKee has designed an experiment for his interns: For 72 hours, they will each be given a particular disease, sleep in hospital beds, eat hospital food, wear hospital gowns, and undergo a battery of medical tests. They will not be doctors; they will be patients. The experiment is a lesson in empathy, as Jack tries to get the interns to view hospital life from the role and perspective of a scared, embarrassed patient.

Discussion Questions:
1. How do you think the interns treated their patients before this experiment? After this experiment?
2. Discuss the differences between a doctor's view and a patient's view of hospital life.
3. Do you think doctors need more empathy for their patients? Is it possible to have too much empathy?
4. How might a similar experiment help communication at your place of work?

Film: Election
Year: 1999
Central Concept: Persuasion
Related Concept: Public Speaking
Approximate Scene Location: 36 minutes into the 103-minute film
Approximate Scene Length: 5 minutes
Opening Line: "We'll move on now to the presidential race"
Closing Line: "Don't vote at all!"

Scene Description: Three candidates are running for student government president at Carver High School: Tracy, Paul, and Tammy. Each is required to give a brief speech at a student assembly. Tracy's presentation is memorized, well-constructed, and delivered with precision and flair (and a dose of overconfidence, which generates crude catcalls from students who think she is stuck up). Paul, a popular athlete, reads his speech directly from his notecards. While his content is solid, he has little or no eye contact, facial expression, or vocal variety—and the students don't know how to respond (they are prompted to applaud by a teacher). Tammy, Paul's sister, thinks that student government is a joke; she is running for election to spite her brother and his girlfriend. She speaks extemporaneously and with passion about the "pathetic" election process and encourages people to either vote for her or not vote at all. She gets a rousing response.

Discussion Questions:
1. Identify the strengths and weaknesses of each of the candidates' speeches.
2. Evaluate the persuasive appeals of each candidate in terms of logos, pathos, and ethos.
3. Which candidate would get your vote—and why?

Film: Finding Forrester
Year: 2000
Central Concept: Perception (Stereotyping)
Related Concepts: Culture, Identity Management
Approximate Scene Location: 18 minutes into the 136-minute film
Approximate Scene Length: 1 minute
Opening Line: "I'm not going to do anything to your car, man"
Closing Line: "No problem, man"

Scene Description: Jamal is an African-American teenager whose intelligence earns him a full scholarship to a prestigious, all-white prep school. He lives, however, in a tough, all-black neighborhood—so he often feels caught between two cultures. In this scene, a white man parks a sporty BMW in Jamal's neighborhood. When Jamal approaches the car, he perceives the driver reacting defensively. The two men have a tense conversation in which Jamal, by demonstrating his knowledge about the BMW company, attempts to disprove any stereotypes the driver might have about him.

Discussion Questions:
1. Describe how and why both the driver and Jamal engage in stereotyping at the outset of this scene. What nonverbal and verbal cues are involved?
2. Explain the role of selection, organization, and interpretation in the perceptions these two men hold of each other. Do their perceptions change as a result of their conversation? If so, how and why?
3. Discuss how the driver and Jamal engage in identity management throughout this scene. Use three words to describe the identity that each man tries to present.

Film: Grease
Year: 1978
Central Concept: Identity Management
Related Concepts: Nonverbal, Communication Competence
Approximate Scene Location: 22 minutes into the 110-minute movie
Approximate Scene Length: 2 minutes
Opening Line: "Hey, Sandy, we've got a surprise for you"
Closing Line: "Sandy, men are rats"

Scene Description: Sandy and Danny spent the summer in a blissful romance (the subject of the hit song, "Summer Nights"). When they parted ways at the end of the season, they thought they would never see each other again. However, Sandy's family moves and she ends up attending Rydell High. When she tells her new friends about her summer fling with a guy named Danny, they figure out that it's the same Danny who attends Rydell—and they set them up for a surprise "re-meeting." When Danny and Sandy first see each other, their faces and voices fill with delight. Quickly, however, Danny realizes he is in front of his hood buddies—and he changes his persona to be tough and cool rather than sensitive and sweet. Sandy is bewildered and devastated that the Danny she knew over the summer is so dramatically different from the Danny at Rydell High.

Discussion Questions:
1. Discuss this scene in terms of identity management. Why does Danny's self-presentation change so dramatically, while Sandy's does not?
2. Discuss the nonverbal messages Danny sends in this scene. When and how does he (and doesn't he) "leak" information about how he really feels?
3. Would you assess Danny as being "phony" or "communicatively competent" in this scene? What is the line of difference between the two? Explain your answer with concepts from the textbook.
4. Have you ever been in a similar situation where you felt "caught" between people you know from very different roles and contexts? How did you handle it?

Film: Gung Ho (Scene 1)
Year: 1986
Central Concept: Culture
Related Concept: Communication Competence
Approximate Scene Location: 8 minutes into the 110-minute film
Approximate Scene Length: 4 minutes
Opening Line: "Hi, fellas" (after entering the building with screen in hand)
Closing Line: "C'mon . . . c'mon" (with head in hands)

Scene Description: A scene reminiscent of "The Ugly American." Hunt Stevenson goes to Japan in an attempt to lure Assan Motors to bring their business to his hometown of Hadleyville. His pitch to the Assan executives is an excellent example of what <u>not</u> to do. Clearly, Stevenson has not analyzed his audience or the setting (e.g., he lugs a projector screen to the session, not realizing that the room in which he is presenting is very high-tech). Moreover, he makes comments that are culturally insensitive (e.g., references to World War II) and interpersonally offensive (e.g., coarse references to women and underwear). The scene is very funny, but it is also uncomfortable. An excellent example for hybrid communication courses that address interpersonal, intercultural, and public speaking competence.

Discussion Questions:
1.   In what ways does Hunt Stevenson exhibit intercultural incompetence?
2.   In what ways does Stevenson demonstrate that he has not analyzed his audience/setting?
3.   How could Stevenson have made this pitch more effectively?

Film: Gung Ho (Scene 2)
Year: 1986
Central Concepts: Culture, Organizational Communication
Related Concept: Persuasion
Approximate Scene Location: 26 minutes into the 110-minute film
Approximate Scene Length: 3 minutes
Opening Line: "Good morning. Welcome to your first day at Assan Motors"
Closing Line: [American workers mocking the Japanese exercises]

Scene Description: Assan Motors has taken over an American auto factory that is on the verge of bankruptcy. The new managers want the American auto laborers to do morning calisthenics, as is the custom at Japanese auto plants. When the American workers resist, a Japanese manager implores, "We must be a team—one, with one purpose only—everyone think only of company." The American workers ignore the manager's plea until Hunt Stevenson, the liaison between the Japanese managers and the American workers, persuades them to do the exercises. The workers do the calisthenics begrudgingly and dance mockingly while they are supposed to be exercising.

Discussion Questions:
1.   Describe how this scene illustrates cultural differences between Japanese and American approaches to working for an organization, using concepts from your textbook.
2.   What persuasive methods does Hunt Stevenson employ to get the American workers to comply with the Japanese manager's directions?

Film: He Said, She Said
Year: 1991
Central Concept: Perception
Related Concepts: Gender, Self-Disclosure, Relational Intimacy, Relational Stages
Approximate Scene Location: 78 minutes into the 115-minute film
Approximate Scene Length: 75 seconds
Opening Line: "Hey" (Lorie) "What?" (Dan) "I love you" (Lorie)
Closing Line: "Really, you don't have to" (Lorie)

Scene Description: *He Said, She Said* tells the story(s) of Lorie's and Dan's relationship from Dan's point of view (directed by Ken Kwapis) and Lorie's point of view (directed by Marisa Silver). This scene is Lorie's account of the first time she tells Dan she loves him. Dan's blank face and speechlessness suggest that he thinks she is becoming too intimate too quickly. Although she claims otherwise, Lorie appears to expect a reciprocal disclosure from Dan—perhaps because she sees their relationship at the integrating stage (while he doesn't). This same scene is told from Dan's point of view at another point in the movie (approximately 38 minutes into the film), illustrating how Lorie and Dan perceive and remember this event differently.

Discussion Questions:
1. What response do you think Lorie was expecting from Dan? Why?
2. At what relational stage does Lorie see their relationship? At what stage does Dan see it?
3. How much of this situation do you think happened exactly as depicted in this scene? How much of the recounting was affected by Lorie's perception and memory?
4. What might Dan's version of this story look/sound like? (This question can be asked before showing Dan's version).
5. What effect does gender have on Dan's and Lorie's perceptions? Do you think this is an accurate portrayal of gender differences?

Film: Japanese Story
Year: 2004
Central Concepts: Language; Paralanguage
Related Concepts: Cultural Norms
Approximate Scene Location: 42:33 into the 99-minute film
Approximate Scene Length: 1 minute
DVD Chapter: Chapter 10: Language Lessons
Opening Line: "I wanted to kill you."
Closing Line: "Even if they mean no?" "Hye."

Scene Description: Australian geologist Sandy Edwards has been assigned to show mining sites to Hiromitsu, a geologist from Japan. Gradually, they learn about each other's cultures. In this scene, Sandy asks Hiromitsu about his frequent use of the Japanese word "hye," and he explains how it can have many different meanings.

Discussion Questions:
1. Hiromitsu says that even though "hye," is literally translated as "yes," it has many meanings, including "no". Use course concepts to explain how this can be true.
2. How is using "hye" to say "no" related to Japan being a collectivist culture?
3. Think of a word in English that has at least three different meanings depending on how you say it. What are the different meanings? What paralinguistic cues are used to change the meanings?

Film: Jerry Maguire
Year: 1997
Central Concept: Relational Intimacy
Related Concepts: Communication Climate, Conflict
Approximate Scene Location: 105 minutes into the 139-minute film
Approximate Scene Length: 3 minutes
Opening Line: "You guys, I go to see this so-called black film . . ." (in the restaurant)
Closing Line: "But that's why you love me, right?"

Scene Description: Jerry and Dorothy recently married each other out of convenience. Although they are husband and wife, they are relationally distant. They are going through the motions of married life, while every other relationship depicted in this scene is, by comparison, more intimate than theirs. Jerry is passionate about his career as a sports agent but has little passion for his wife. As a result, he sends her a variety of disconfirming messages (some verbal, some nonverbal) in their bedroom discussion.

Discussion Questions:
1. Describe the levels of intimacy in the various relationships depicted in this scene. Rate and rank them, using 10 for a highly intimate relationship and 1 for a non-intimate relationship.
2. Describe the communication climate in Jerry's bedroom discussion with Dorothy. What factors from Gibb's climate model are evident in their interaction?
3. Identify the conflict style(s) employed by Jerry.
4. How might Jerry convey his thoughts, feelings, and wants more effectively to Dorothy?

Film: Joy Luck Club, The (Scene 1)
Year: 1993
Central Concept: Culture
Related Concept: Communication Competence
Approximate Scene Location: 43 minutes into the 138-minute film
Approximate Scene Length: 4 minutes
Opening Line: "The next week I brought Rich to Mom's birthday dinner" (Waverly's voice)
Closing Line: "All this needs is a little soy sauce"

Scene Description: Waverly, a Chinese-American woman, brings her Anglo-American boyfriend Rich home for a dinner cooked by her Chinese mother, Lindo. Rich unknowingly insults Waverly's family when he fails to follow the rules of Chinese dining. For instance, he shocks everyone at the table by taking a large first serving of the entree. As Waverly explains in her narration, it is customary in Chinese culture to take only a small spoonful of a dish until everyone else has had some. Rich's biggest mistake is when he misunderstands Lindo's description of her prized entree. Lindo says, "This dish no good. Too salty." Rich decodes the message literally, not paying attention to Lindo's nonverbal cues. The family knows that when Lindo insults her cooking, it means she is pleased with it. The implicit rule is to eat some, then compliment it profusely. Instead, Rich floods the prized dish with soy sauce and assures Lindo that it is not beyond repair.

Discussion Questions:
1. What differences between American and Chinese cultures are depicted in this scene? Use terms from lecture and text in your analysis.
2. What could Rich have done to enhance his intercultural competence?

Film: Joy Luck Club, The (Scene 2)
Year: 1993
Central Concept: Conflict
Related Concept: Self-Concept
Approximate Scene Location: 90 minutes into the 139-minute film
Approximate Scene Length: 2 minutes
Opening Line: "Honey, should we eat in or out tonight?" (Rose)
Closing Line: "Are you happy?" (Ted) "Of course I am" (Rose)

Scene Description: Rose asks her husband Ted what he wants for dinner that night. "You decide," he answers. Rose's responses of "Oh, I don't care," "You've had a hard day," and "I just want you to be happy" reveal her accommodating style of dealing with conflict. She has silenced her opinions in their marriage and has lost her sense of identity. Ted is frustrated by his wife's lack of input and wants some productive conflict. "I'd like to hear your voice, even if we disagree," he says. "You used to have an opinion. We used to argue." The fight leads them to discuss marital separation. (Note: Rose begins to stand up for herself later in the movie and they restore their relationship.)

Discussion Questions:
1. Which style of conflict management does Rose employ in this scene?
2. Why might Rose have chosen this style of conflict management?
3. Why does Ted become upset with Rose?
4. Can a person be too giving? Why or why not?

Film: Liar Liar
Year: 1997
Central Concepts: Honesty, Identity Management
Related Concept: Communication Competence
Approximate Scene Location: 45 minutes into the 87-minute film
Approximate Scene Length: 3 minutes
Opening Line: "Nice to see you Fletcher...would you follow me please?"
Closing Line: "Keep your eyes on that boy, dickhead!"

Scene Description: Fletcher Reede is a fast-talking attorney--and a habitual liar. He has misused the concept of identity management to justify dishonesty in his personal and business affairs. Reede's five-year-old son wishes that his father cannot tell a lie for just one day, and miraculously the wish comes true. In this scene, Reede's boss calls him into a boardroom meeting to speak to the director of the partnership committee. Because of his son's wish, Reede begins saying whatever comes to mind. His unedited thoughts and feelings lead to rude and insulting comments about everyone in the room. After a few moments of uncertainty and silence, the head of the partnership committee breaks out in laughter, thinking it is a joke, and encourages Reede to continue. The director says, "He loves a good roast!" [Warning: this scene contains some coarse language]

Discussion Questions:
1. In what ways does Fletcher Reede exhibit communication incompetence?
2. How could/should Reede have expressed himself at the meeting? Would it be unethical for him not to share his honest thoughts and feelings?
3. Reede's insensitive disclosures at this meeting received laughter and endorsement. What would be a more likely reaction in a real-life scenario?
4. What does this scene suggest about the famous maxim, "Honesty is always the best policy"?

Film: Love Actually
Year: 2003
Central Concepts: Nonverbal (Deception and Leakage)
Related Concepts: Ethics of Deception
Approximate Scene Location: 28:16 into the 135-minute film
Approximate Scene Length: 1 minute, 30 seconds
DVD Chapter: Four (6 minutes into chapter)
Opening Line: "So, what's the problem?"
Closing Line: "You're right. Total agony."

Scene Description: Daniel (Liam Neeson) is very worried about his eleven-year-old stepson, Sam (Thomas Sangster). Sam's mother died recently and he has spent nearly all his time alone in his room, leading Daniel to wonder if Sam is using drugs. In this scene, Daniel learns that Sam's "problem" is that he is in love. Daniel is delighted that drugs are not the issue, but he quickly realizes that Sam is taking this puppy love very seriously—and as a result, Daniel attempts to mask the relief and elation he is feeling.

Discussion Questions:
1. Daniel is trying to hide his happiness from Sam, but he is having a hard time doing it. What indications of leakage (showing his true feelings) do you see in Daniel?
2. Why do you think Daniel feels the need to hide his feelings of joy from Sam?
3. Daniel is trying to lie about his feelings. Do you think it's wrong for Daniel to deceive Sam in this manner? Explain your answer.

Film: Mean Girls
Year: 2004
Central Concept: Communication Climate
Related Concepts: Conflict, Empathy
Approximate Scene Location: 1:10 into the 1:36 film
Approximate Scene Length: 5:34
DVD Chapter: 15 (1:52 into chapter)
Opening Line: "Ms. Norbury, you're a successful, caring, intelligent, graceful young woman."
Closing Line: "Suck on that. Aye yie yie yie!" (as she falls backward to be caught by the other girls)

Scene Description: The girls of the junior class at North Shore High School are constantly in conflict. The disagreements, disconfirmation, and backstabbing (including mean evaluations written in a scrapbook called a "Burn Book") reach a breaking point when the fighting nearly leads to a riot. In response, the school principal calls all the junior girls to the gym where one of the school's teachers, Ms. Norbury, leads them in an "attitude makeover."

Discussion Questions:
1. What is Ms. Norbury's purpose with the two exercises she does where the girls close their eyes? How does it enhance the communication climate and empathy level among the girls?
2. Ms. Norbury says, "You all have got to stop calling each other sluts and whores. It just makes it okay for guys to call you sluts and whores." Do you agree with her assessment? Discuss in terms of course concepts.
3. What style(s) of conflict management does Ms. Norbury use? Is the approach effective in this situation? Discuss how well this approach would (or wouldn't) work in other conflict situations.

Film: Mona Lisa Smile (Scene 1)
Year: 2003
Central Concept: Reasons For Lying
Related Concepts: Effects of Lies
Approximate Scene Location: 44 minutes into the 120-minute film
Approximate Scene Length: 1 minute
DVD Chapter: Chapter 12: Betty's Wedding (the last one minute of the chapter)
Opening Line: "You ready?"
Closing Line: "I know."

Scene Description: This film follows art history professor Katherine Watson as she takes a new job at Wellesley College. She rents a room from speech professor Nancy Abbey, and they become friends. Nancy shares early in the film that she had been engaged, but her fiancé, Lenny, was killed in a World War II battle. In this scene she admits, under the influence of alcohol, that he was not killed. He left her for another woman. Katherine responds sympathetically. [Note: This scene can be used in tandem with the scene described below, in which Katherine does not respond sympathetically when she finds out about a lie she's been told]

Discussion Questions:
1. What is Nancy's reason for telling the lie? How does this reason affect Katherine's reaction to it?
2. In your experience, how does the perceived reason for telling a lie affect the way receivers respond when they detect this dishonesty?
3. To what degree does drinking alcohol increase the likelihood that a person will disclose something he/she wouldn't if sober? Support your answer.

Film: Mona Lisa Smile (Scene 2)
Year: 2003
Central Concept: Effects of Lies
Related Concepts: Reasons For Lying, Identity Management
Approximate Scene Location: 97 minutes (1:37) into the 120-minute film
Approximate Scene Length: 4 minutes
DVD Chapter: Chapter 25: Stan Sher
Opening Line: "Bill, the brochures, the order arrived."
Closing Line: "I think you came to Wellesley to help people find your way."

Scene Description: Art history professor Katherine Watson has developed a romantic relationship with Italian professor and World War II veteran Bill Dunbar. Bill has told Katherine and his students that he fought in Italy during the war. In this scene, Katherine has just learned that Bill never left the US during his service. She responds by terminating the relationship. [Note: This scene can be used in tandem with the scene described above, in which Katherine responds sympathetically when she finds out about a lie she's been told]

Discussion Questions:
1. What was Bill's reason for telling this lie?
2. How did Bill's reason for telling the lie affect Katherine's reaction to it?
3. Bill tries to defend himself by explaining that he didn't create the lie, but that others assumed this part of his background and he simply didn't correct them. Do you think this is a legitimate defense? Why or why not?
4. Are lies ever ethically acceptable? Explain your answer, giving examples.

Film: My Family
Year: 1995
Central Concept: Culture
Related Concepts: Communication Climate, Communication Competence, Family Communication
Approximate Scene Location: 105 minutes into the 120-minute film
Approximate Scene Length: 4 minutes
Opening Line: "And he had the chance of his lifetime one Sunday . . ." (narrator's voice)
Closing Line: "C'mon, c'mon" (trying to calm things down)

Scene Description: This is essentially a Mexican-American "Guess Who's Coming to Dinner" scene. In a poor but happy Mexican-American family, son Memo (short for Guillermo) has made it big as a successful lawyer. He brings his Anglo fiancée Karen and her parents to his parents' humble home to meet his family. As the narrator describes, although Karen had been born and raised in L.A., "she had never been to East L.A." Several cultures come face-to-face in the scene: Mexican and Anglo, urban and suburban, poor and rich. The meeting is cordial but uncomfortable—particularly for Memo, who is caught between cultures. Although his heritage is Mexican, he clearly identifies with the dress, language, and behavior of the upper-class Anglo culture to which he has become accustomed. As he explains to Karen's parents, "I've never been to Mexico. I've always lived here in Los Angeles, just like yourselves." Memo's distancing of himself from his Mexican heritage infuriates his brother Jimmy, who perceives it as a put-down and becomes defensive. The scene ends with yelling, apologies, and embarrassment.

Discussion Questions:
1. What are the cultural differences between Memo's family and Karen's family?
2. Which characters exhibit intercultural and communicative competence? Which do not?
3. What is the communication climate between Jimmy and Memo? What factors lead to this climate? How could this climate be changed?

Film: O Brother, Where Art Thou?
Year: 2001
Central Concept: Group Communication
Approximate Scene Location: 1.5 minutes
Approximate Scene Length: 4 minutes into the 103-minute film
Opening Line: Three chain-gang convicts running toward a moving train (no dialogue at this point)
Closing Line: "I'm with you fellas"

Scene Description: Three escaped convicts are on the run from a 1930s Louisiana chain gang. They are linked together and attempt to board a moving train. Two of the convicts successfully leap into a boxcar, but the third one can't make the jump—so all of them tumble out of the train. The convicts then begin to make plans about what to do next. Immediately, there is a squabble about leadership and decision-making. They take a vote, which ends in an amusing draw. This brief scene could make a provocative discussion starter for a section (or a course) on small group communication. Instructors can show the clip, then ask the general question, "What does this scene illustrate about working in groups?" The answers could range from "What affects one person affects everybody in the group" (the convicts' chains are a wonderful metaphor for interdependence), to "Everyone wants to know who's in charge," to "A group is only as strong as its weakest link" (there are numerous possible responses involving consensus, decision-making, vote-taking, power resources, etc.).

Discussion Question:
1. What does this scene illustrate about working together in groups?

Film: Office Space (Scene 1)
Year: 1999
Central Concept: Communication Climate
Related Concepts: Listening, Emotions, Nonverbal
Approximate Scene Location: 3 minutes into 88-minute film
Approximate Scene Length: 5 minutes
Opening Line: Peter walking through the office door as the film credits roll
Closing Line: "Yes, I have the memo!"

Scene Description: From the minute Peter walks in the office on Monday morning at Initech, it is clear that he hates his mundane, dehumanizing job. One of the reasons is the way he is treated by his boss, Lumbergh, who approaches him and asks, "What's happening?" It is a counterfeit question because he really doesn't want to know how Peter is doing, nor is he looking for any small talk about the weekend. Instead, he wants to confront Peter about a small mistake in his TPS report. He delivers a patronizing monologue to Peter in a calm, syrupy tone of voice—and shows no interest in Peter's explanation of the problem. After Lumbergh walks away, two other managers confront Peter about the same problem, using the same patronizing tone and lack of listening skills.

Discussion Questions:
1. Describe the communication climate between Peter and his managers. What factors from Gibb's climate model are evident in their interactions?
2. Discuss the managers' listening responses, both verbal and nonverbal, using terms from your textbook.
3. The managers in this scene use calm voices and avoid angry words, yet Peter still feels like he is being "yelled at." Explain how and why this is the case. How might the bosses have communicated their messages more effectively?
4. Watch this scene with the volume turned off. Attempt to describe what the characters are thinking and feeling simply by monitoring their nonverbal cues.

Film: Office Space (Scene 2)
Year: 1999
Central Concept: Communication Climate
Related Concepts: Language, Listening, Perception
Approximate Scene Location: 37 minutes into the 88-minute film
Approximate Scene Length: 1 minute
Opening Line: "Joanna, can I talk to you for a minute?"
Closing Line: "Some people choose to wear more; you do want to express yourself, don't you?"

Scene Description: Joanna is a waitress at Chotchkie's, a restaurant in the mold of Friday's and Bennigan's. Her manager is less than happy with her performance and calls her aside for a pep talk. Unfortunately, he creates a defensive communication climate by sending messages that are, to use Gibb's terms, evaluative, controlling, strategic, neutral, and superior. The manager is ambiguous and indirect as he talks to Joanna about her "flair" (a euphemism meant to describe the environment of fun at Chotchkie's, but something he measures by the number of buttons on her uniform). He also sends her negative nonverbal messages through a patronizing tone of voice and by rolling his eyes. Instead of describing what he wants from her, he asks impersonal and counterfeit questions such as, "What do you think of a person that only does the bare minimum?" and "Some people choose to wear more [flair buttons]; you do want to express yourself, don't you?"

Discussion Questions:
1. What is the communication climate between Joanna and her manager? What verbal and nonverbal messages are factors in the creating that climate?
2. Give examples of how the manager's language illustrates the concepts of vagueness, abstraction, and euphemisms. Describe how he could convey his concerns more precisely, concretely, and constructively.

3. Discuss how the manager uses counterfeit questioning in his listening responses. How could he have asked the same questions more sincerely?
4. Joanna attempts to use perception checking to clarify her manager's request. What effect does this have on their communication, and why?

Film: One True Thing
Year: 1998
Central Concept: Family Communication
Related Concept: Communication Climate
Approximate Scene Location: About 29 minutes into the 127-minute film
Approximate Scene Length: About 2.5 minutes
Opening Line: "I'm glad you're home"
Closing Line: "Thanks for taking care of this"

Scene Description: Freelance writer Ellen Gulden grew up idolizing her father George, a self-important professor and literary critic. Ellen comes home for a surprise birthday party honoring George and soon learns that her mother is stricken with cancer. This scene takes place in George's study, where he invites Ellen to write the introduction to a volume of his collected essays. At first she is deeply honored by what she takes as a measure of her father's respect for her professional talent. But immediately after flattering Ellen with his offer, George dashes her spirits by heaping her arms full of soiled shirts and tossing off instructions on how to launder them.

Discussion Questions:
1. Describe the insights this scene offers into this family's system of operation. What seem to be the typical roles and relationships of the father, daughter, and (non-pictured) mother? How do the family members handle changes in the system?
2. Discuss the climate and the messages in this scene in terms of the following pairs of concepts: content/relationship; confirming/disconfirming; verbal/nonverbal; equality/superiority.

Film: Philadelphia
Year: 1993
Central Concept: Communication Climate
Related Concepts: Perception, Nonverbal
Approximate Scene Location: 22 minutes into the 119-minute film
Approximate Scene Length: 2 minutes
Opening Line: "Look, I want you to explain this to me like I'm a 6-year old"
Closing Line: "What can I do for you?" (Note: Clip ends in the middle of their conversation)

Scene Description: This scene illustrates how quickly a communication climate can change from warm to cold. Attorney Joe Miller establishes a friendly, confirming climate within his office, as we see him provide assistance and reassurance to one of his clients. Miller then welcomes his next client, Andrew Beckett, with a broad smile and a firm handshake. However, when Beckett reveals that he has AIDS, the climate in the room instantly becomes cold and uncomfortable. Miller's perceptions of the disease and stereotypes of those who have it are obvious in his disconfirming verbal and nonverbal cues.

Discussion Questions:
1. Describe the communication climate in the office before and after Beckett reveals that he has AIDS. Identify specific verbal and nonverbal cues that lead to your conclusions.
2. What are Miller's perceptions of people who have AIDS? What are some of the factors that may have contributed to his perceptions?
3. Discuss the possibilities of steering this communication climate from negative back to positive.

Film: Pretty Woman
Year: 1990
Central Concept: Self-Concept
Approximate Scene Location: 60 minutes into the 119-minute film
Approximate Scene Length: 2 minutes
Opening Line: "The first guy I ever loved was a total nothing . . ."
Closing Line: "You ever notice that?"

Scene Description: In this scene, Vivian shares her story with Edward of how she became a call girl. Her history with men, previous jobs, and prostitution suggests that she has low self-esteem and has molded her self-concept from the negative appraisals of others. Even when Edward tells Vivian that she has potential, she says, "People put you down enough times, you start to believe it." The experiences of her life make it difficult for Vivian to see herself as worthwhile.

Discussion Questions:
1. How is Vivian's self-concept related to reflected appraisal?
2. Why is it that "the bad stuff is easier to believe" when forming a self-concept?
3. How might Vivian's occupation play a role in forming and perpetuating her self-concept?

Film: Reality Bites
Year: 1994
Central Concept: Relational Stages
Related Concept: Self-Disclosure
Approximate Scene Location: 40 minutes into 119-minute film
Approximate Scene Length: 5 minutes
Opening Line: "Oh my God; are you a collection agent?"
Closing Line: "Like right now" (before kissing) "Yeah, right now"

Scene Description: Lelaina and Michael are on their first date. During their evening together, they experience several relational stages—although not necessarily in the "correct" sequence. They begin their dinner in the experimenting stage, then abruptly move into topics usually associated with the intensifying stage (e.g., Michael gushes that Lelaina is beautiful; Lelaina says she is a "non-practicing virgin"). They seem a bit uncomfortable with these sudden, intimate disclosures, so they "retreat" to experimenting talk while sitting in Michael's car. By the end of the scene, the relationship is intensifying once again—but this time less awkwardly.

Discussion Questions:
1. What relational stages do Michael and Lelaina experience in this scene?
2. Is it possible to experience relational stages "out of order?" Is it important (or necessary) to take relational stages in "correct" order?
3. Which of their self-disclosures seem appropriate for their level of relationship? Which of their self-disclosures seem inappropriate?
4. How are these two similar? How are they different? Why are they attracted to each other?

Film: Remains of the Day, The
Year: 1993
Central Concept: Nonverbal
Related Concepts: Relational Intimacy, Relational Dialectics, Emotions
Approximate Scene Location: 87 minutes into the 135-minute film
Approximate Scene Length: 3 minutes
Opening Line: "Flowers" (Miss Kenton) "Hmm?" "Flowers."
Closing Line: "I really must ask you please not to disturb the few moments I have to myself"

Scene Description: *The Remains of the Day* focuses on the 1930's working relationship between Stevens, a reserved and proper head butler of a huge English mansion, and Miss Kenton, the mansion's outspoken housekeeper. Stevens has learned to repress his emotions, which becomes obvious when Kenton surprises him in his den as he is reading. She invades his personal time and space, especially as she inches nearer and nearer to him. Kenton and Stevens have developed romantic feelings for one another, but Stevens's inability to express his emotions makes this situation uncomfortable, even painful, for the two of them (as well as for the audience). Does Stevens want Kenton to leave him alone, as his words command, or does he wish that she would spend this quiet moment with him, as his eyes suggest? The contradiction between Stevens' verbal and nonverbal communication points to the dialectical tension of intimacy/distance at work in their relationship.

Discussion Questions:
1. Discuss the nonverbal messages being exchanged in this scene, using terms from this course.
2. Discuss the mixed messages in this scene. How and when do the content messages contradict the relationship messages?
3. What dialectical tensions are in evidence between Stevens and Kenton?
4. How did you feel as you watched this scene? Identify three specific emotions.

Film: Story of Us, The
Year: 2000
Central Concepts: Self-Concept, Family
Related Concepts: Perception, Emotions
Approximate Scene Location: 37 minutes into the 97-minute film
Approximate Scene Length: 3 minutes
Opening Line: "When two people go to bed, there are actually six people in that bed"
Closing Line: "F--- you!"

Scene Description: Ben and Katie Jordan are seeing yet another marriage counselor for their struggling marriage. The counselor in this scene explains that when they go to bed with each other, they are actually going to bed with their parents as well (i.e., the influence of their parents is always with them, even at intimate moments). Katie and Ben begin to argue about whether or not to have sex—and suddenly, their parents (imaginarily) appear in bed with them. The arguing among the various couples offers clues about the issues that both the parents and their children face in their relationships. [A word of warning: The scene ends with Katie shouting, "F--- you!" Depending upon the audience, this moment in the scene could be included, cut, or dubbed over].

Discussion Questions:
1. Describe how this scene illustrates the role of reflected appraisal and social comparison in forming a person's self-concept.
2. Discuss how Ben and Katie could use the textbook material on Emotions to process their thoughts and feelings about these matters.
3. Based on what you hear from their parents, how do you think Katie and Ben perceive marriage, intimacy, and relationships?
4. Describe how this scene illustrates the notion that "The apple doesn't fall far from the tree.

Film: Truth About Cats and Dogs, The
Year: 1996
Central Concept: Self-Concept
Related Concepts: Nonverbal, Gender
Approximate Scene Location: 81 minutes into the 97-minute film
Approximate Scene Length: 4 minutes
Opening Line: "Donna, where's Abby?"
Closing Line: "You're dumb and beautiful and you're smart and . . ."

Scene Description: Dr. Abby Barnes, a savvy, witty veterinarian who hosts her own radio show, is anything but confident when it comes to dating. Because of her lack of self-esteem regarding her appearance, Abby convinces a love-struck caller (Brian) who has never seen her that she is a tall, thin beautiful blonde. In this scene, Brian doesn't know that the short brunette to whom he is talking is actually Abby. The conversation is painful as it becomes clear that Brian loves the idea of Abby rather than Abby herself. (Note: Instructors will need to "set the scene" to use this clip.)

Discussion Questions:
1.   What does this scene suggest about Abby's self-concept in romantic relationships?
2.   Discuss how this scene could contribute to a self-fulfilling prophecy for Abby.
3.   How might Brian's final line affect Abby's self-concept? Will she hear the message positively or negatively?
4.   Does our culture place too much value on physical attractiveness in interpersonal relationships? Are there different standards for men and women?

Film: White Man's Burden
Year: 1995
Central Concept: Perception (Stereotyping and Empathy)
Related Concept: Culture
Approximate Scene Location: Beginning of the 90-minute movie
Approximate Scene Length: 2 minutes
Opening Line: "I would like to propose a toast"
Closing Line: "The bottom line is a very simple question: Are these a people who are beyond being helped?"

Scene Description: This movie attempts to portray and expose common racial stereotypes by depicting a society in which black people are the upper-class majority and white people are the lower-class minority. The movie's opening scene is a dinner party in which well-to-do black people are being waited on by a white maid. Stereotypes and generalizations are made about white people, but it is likely that viewers won't realize the film's agenda until the end of the scene. It might be useful to show the scene a second time, allowing viewers to reassess their first impressions.

Discussion Questions:
1.   What were your first impressions of the dinner guests and their comments? Did your impressions change by the end of the scene? How might your impressions and interpretations change upon viewing the scene a second time?
2.   What statements at the dinner party are rooted in stereotypes, generalizations, and prejudices?
3.   How and why might a viewer's empathy be increased by watching this scene (and movie)?

SECTION II
FULL-LENGTH FEATURE FILMS

Each of the film entries in this section provides information in the following categories:

Film Data: Year, Director, Length, and Rating
Characters/Actors: Principal roles in the film
Communication Courses: Appropriate classes for using the film (listed alphabetically)
Communication Concepts: Primary communication topics in the film (listed alphabetically)
Discussion Questions: Questions (and answers to the first two) linking the film to communication concepts

The following are a number of films that have human communication as a central theme. The discussion questions that follow the basic "data" about the film are the heart of this section. The questions posed are not the only ones that can or should be asked, nor are the answers given for the first two films the only "right" way to respond to the questions. In fact, you may argue with some of the analyses and interpretations. That's fine—any good discussion about movies should engender disagreement. The questions (and answers) are provided simply to offer an example of how to analyze the film and the communication that goes on within it.

BETRAYAL

Film Data
Year: 1983
Director: David Jones
Length: 95 minutes
Rated: R

Characters/Actors
Jerry: Jeremy Irons
Robert: Ben Kingsley
Emma: Patricia Hodge

Communication Courses
Family Communication
Interpersonal Communication

Communication Concepts
Emotions
Honesty/Lying
Relational Stages

Pedagogical Perspective
This British film, based on a Harold Pinter play, is designed for adult audiences. The story moves slowly and there is far more talk than action. The dialogue is stilted, which is part of the film's intrigue. The characters' emotions are rarely expressed directly; instead, they are communicated through double entendre, nonverbal cues, and symbolism. This can make the plot difficult to follow at times. Moreover, the story is painful without reprieve. Some consider this a "spinach" movie—you may not enjoy it, but it is good for you. It is a film that can make a profound impact on a viewer, sometimes months after viewing the film.

Synopsis
Betrayal is the story of an ill-fated affair between Emma (Hodge) and Jerry (Irons). Emma is married to Robert (Kingsley), who is Jerry's best friend. Jerry is also married, but his wife never appears on screen in this three-person story. The affair lasts for seven years. Robert learns of (and gets Emma to confess to) the affair five years after it begins. Jerry, however, does not learn that Robert knew about the affair until two years after it has ended.
This is where the film begins—two years after the affair is over. The movie's twist is that it chronicles the story in reverse. Each scene moves backward in time, leading ultimately to the movie's final scene, which depicts the affair's beginning. The viewers thus know the outcome of the characters' choices before the characters do. This omniscient viewpoint makes the movie ideal for relationship analysis.

Discussion Questions with Sample Answers

1. How does Emma and Jerry's affair illustrate Knapp's stages of relational development and deterioration?
In the last scene of the movie, which is the beginning of the affair, Jerry and Emma move quickly from platonic friendship to the intensifying stage of a romantic relationship. They cover quite a bit of territory in a matter of minutes. This is due in part to Jerry's drunkenness, which leads him to a level of experimenting that he probably would not have ventured if he were sober. While a party goes on at Emma and Robert's home, Jerry waits for Emma in her bedroom. She comes in to comb her hair and Jerry begins showering her with compliments. He tells her, "I've been waiting for you...you're beautiful. I've been watching you all night." Emma acts surprised and

confused by his comments and believes his behavior is only the wine talking. At the same time, she relishes the attention—perhaps because her husband Robert is a detached and non-expressive person.

Jerry continues to gush over Emma, then touches her arm. As she tries to pull away, Jerry plunges into the intensifying stage, typified by the direct expression of feelings. "You're lovely, I'm crazy about you," Jerry declares. "All these words I'm saying, don't you see they've never been said before, can't you see?" But Emma doesn't see, and she reminds Jerry that Robert is just outside the door. Jerry is undaunted: "I love you, I adore you. I'm madly in love with you." Emma attempts to resist, but eventually gives in to his kiss. The scene—and the movie—ends with a picture of their joined hands, their wedding rings clearly visible. For the viewers, who know the affair will lead to a broken marriage and a damaged friendship, the symbolism is chilling.

Their relationship continues to intensify as they secretly call one another and meet for afternoon rendezvous. To make their meetings more convenient and frequent, they decide to rent a flat. This marks their transition into the integrating stage. "Their" flat, the tablecloth Emma buys for "their home," and the bed they purchase all suggest that they see themselves as a couple. Their problem, however, is that the natural next stage in their relationship would be bonding. During the bonding stage, certain public gestures typically occur, such as getting married or moving in together. Jerry and Emma cannot do this (except under assumed names) because they both are already married. On one occasion at the flat, Emma raises this issue. She asks Jerry, "Have you ever thought about changing your life?" He quickly answers, "It's impossible." The clear implication is that their relationship will never be more than a secret affair. Their inability (or unwillingness) to go public puts a limit on their relational development.

Because their relationship stalls at the integrating stage, they begin to differentiate. They already lead two separate lives, which makes it difficult to maintain commitment to their affair—particularly once the thrill of intensifying/integrating has worn off. The stress of keeping their affair a secret also takes its toll. After Robert discovers their affair, Emma in effect betrays Jerry by not telling him that Robert knows. This secret, and the growing infrequency of their meetings, suggests the stages of circumscribing, stagnating, and avoiding.

Evidence of these stages can be seen and heard in Jerry and Emma's discussion when they meet in the flat for the last time. As they stand at a distance, Emma asks, "Can you actually remember when we were last here?" Jerry replies, "Well things have changed. You've been so busy with you're job and everything...you're not free in the afternoon, are you? So how can we meet?" Emma realizes this is an indicator of passion lost and says, "In the past, we were inventive, we were determined. It seemed impossible to meet, and yet we did. We met in this flat because we wanted to." She looks around the flat and sees the items that once represented love; but the bed, tablecloth, and curtains now disgust her. She says, "It's just an empty home." Jerry reminds her it is not a home. Emma realizes that she and Jerry probably had different expectations of their relationship and says, "You didn't ever see it as a home in any sense, did you?" Jerry answers, "No, I saw it as a flat, you know . . . for loving." Emma coldly replies, "Well there's not much of that left, is there?" Their reminiscing suggests they have reached the terminating stage; they make it official by discussing how to handle selling the flat. Emma returns her key, leaves the flat, and cries alone in her car.

2. How do lies affect the characters' relationships?

Robert is the first victim of lies in this story when his wife and his best friend betray him by having an affair. Robert becomes extremely bitter upon learning of the affair. Instead of discussing it with Emma or confronting Jerry, he punishes them both with mental, verbal, and nonverbal games. He uses information as a source of power and lack of self-disclosure as a source of control. He doesn't tell Jerry that he knows about the affair; instead, he watches Jerry squirm as he plays cat-and-mouse with him during lunch at a restaurant and later during a living room conversation. Robert also begins cheating on Emma, and by the end of the story they decide to divorce.

Emma and Jerry's affair begins to decline after Emma returns from a vacation in Italy. Robert learns of the affair from Emma during the vacation, but she does not disclose this to Jerry when she comes home. She also lies to Jerry about vacation events to keep him learning the secret. Jerry later learns that she lied but decides not to confront her. Ultimately, everyone lies and holds secrets from everyone else—and all their relationships are injured or destroyed as a result.

BOYZ N THE HOOD

Film Data
Year: 1991
Director: John Singleton
Length: 112 minutes
Rated: R

Characters/Actors
Tre Styles: Cuba Gooding
Doughboy: Ice Cube
Ricky Baker: Morris Chestnut
Furious (Fury) Styles: Lawrence Fishburne
Brandi: Nira Long
Mrs. Baker: Tyra Ferrell
Reva Styles: Angela Bassett

Communication Courses
Family Communication
Interpersonal Communication

Communication Concepts
Communication Climate
Conflict
Self-Concept

Pedagogical Perspective
This is a powerful movie that offers an important glimpse into a world that is rarely depicted in Hollywood films. The language is rough and the violence is graphic, but so are the streets of South Central Los Angeles. *Boyz* takes place in a black, urban, crime-ridden neighborhood and involves a stark depiction of family life, illustrating the power of confirming/disconfirming communication.

Synopsis
Boyz N the Hood offers a rare glimpse into the mean streets of (and friendships within) a South Central Los Angeles neighborhood. Tre (Gooding), Doughboy (Ice Cube), and Ricky (Chestnut) become lifelong pals after Tre moves into the neighborhood to live with his father, Furious "Fury" Styles (Fishburne). Ricky and Doughboy, half brothers being raised by a single mother, choose different paths while growing up. Doughboy's life is filled with crime, gang life, and "hangin' out." Ricky is a star football player who pursues a college scholarship as a ticket out of "the hood." Tre is a model of strength and character, due in large part to his father's guidance. Fury disciplines, mentors, and befriends Tre; as a result, Tre has a solid personal and moral foundation.

Although the story is set on a pleasant-looking street, the threat of gangs, drugs, and violence is ever-present (particularly at night, when the streets become a war zone). At several points in the movie, Fury offers compelling arguments about the problems of (and solutions for) their neighborhood and their culture. Ricky, who listens to and respects Tre's dad, nevertheless becomes a victim of a gang shooting. Ricky's murder pushes Tre to the brink; he wants revenge for his best friend's death. Instead, he takes the high road and walks away. The movie's endnotes declare what would be easy to guess: Doughboy becomes another victim of "the hood," while Tre goes on to college.

Discussion Questions

1. Discuss the differences in Tre's, Ricky's, and Doughboy's self-concepts. Explain how they are affected by reflected appraisal and confirming/disconfirming messages.

Tre's strong self-concept is a reflection of his parents' positive appraisal—particularly his father's. Even when Fury disciplines Tre, he sends the message that he cares about and loves his son. "I'm trying to teach you how to be responsible," Fury explains, "unlike your little friends across the street. They don't have anybody to show them how to do that." In a warning that proves to be prophetic, he concludes, "You're gonna see how they end up, too."

In another scene, Fury takes Tre on a walk and asks him if he is a leader or a follower. When Tre says he is a leader, Fury asks him to recite the "three rules." Tre responds, "Always look a person in the eye. Do that, they respect you better. Two was to never be afraid to ask you [Fury] for anything . . . The last one, I think, was to never respect anyone that doesn't respect you back." Fury is pleased that his son has remembered his fatherly advice. As Fury notes later, and the movie bears out, "Any fool with a dick can make a baby, but only a real man can raise his children."

Ricky has a relatively strong self-concept, due in part to the many confirming messages he receives from his mother. "I always knew you would amount to something," Mrs. Baker tells Ricky. "You make your mama proud." Unfortunately, she doesn't provide Ricky with the same guidance that Tre receives from his father. Toward this end, Ricky looks to Furious and Tre for mentoring and they become significant in shaping his view of the world. Ricky receives some lessons directly from Fury, such as when Furious explains the problem of gentrification ("Furious is deep," Ricky exclaims at the end of Fury's impromptu sermon).

In contrast to Ricky and Tre, Doughboy is subjected to negative appraisals from a young age. Mrs. Baker tells him, "You ain't shit— you're just like your daddy. You don't do shit, and you ain't never gonna amount to shit." The prediction becomes a self-fulfilling prophecy for Doughboy. Even his friends notice that Ricky receives preferential treatment. After Mrs. Baker yells at Doughboy, they observe, "She ain't like that with Rick. It's because they've got different daddies."

When Ricky and Doughboy get into a fight, Mrs. Baker slaps Doughboy but doesn't say or do anything to Ricky. After Ricky gets shot and Doughboy brings his body back to the house, Mrs. Baker pushes Doughboy aside to get to Ricky, then turns and yells to Doughboy, "What did you do? You did this! You did this!" At the end of the movie, Doughboy laments to Tre: "I don't got no brother. Got no mother, neither. She loved that fool more than she loved me." Doughboy's self-concept is shaped by negative appraisals, comparisons with his brother, and pessimistic prophecies.

2. Discuss the reasons for, and approaches to, conflict in "the hood."

Wilmot's definition of conflict is "an expressed struggle between at least two interdependent parties who perceive incompatible goals, scarce rewards, and interference from the other party in achieving their goals." In the gang wars of "the hood," scarce rewards and interference from the other party are central to the never-ending conflicts. Money is tight; upper mobility is limited; turf is small. As a result, drugs and guns offer quick (and shortsighted) rewards of cash and power. Violence begets violence in an ever-escalating cycle of destruction. When a gang shooting takes place, the immediate response is to seek and gain revenge—which costs both Ricky and Doughboy their lives.

Fury's goal is to help the members of the black community see, understand, and appreciate their interdependence. As he explains to Ricky, "It's the 90's. We can't afford to be afraid of our own people anymore." Furious is upset when Tre tells him he should have blown off the head of a black man who attempted to rob their house. Fury says, "Don't say that. Just would have been contributing to killing another brother." An African-American policeman who investigates the crime agrees that the robber should have been shot, because it "would be one less nigger out on the streets we would have to worry about." Fury looks at the policeman with disdain; the policeman challenges him by asking "Is something wrong?" Fury responds, "Yeah. It's just too bad you don't know what it is . . . brother."

The concept of black brotherhood as a means to "increase the peace" is also the theme of an impromptu sermon that Fury offers to a group of listeners in a vacant lot. "What we need to do is keep everything in our neighborhood, everything black. Black owned with black money. . . . They [the white establishment] want us to kill ourselves. The best way you can destroy a people is if you take away their ability to reproduce themselves. Who is out here dying on the streets every night? You all. Young brothers like yourself." Furious wants his neighborhood and his culture to handle their conflicts more functionally through cooperation, de-escalation, and foresightedness. Tre heeds Fury's call: He walks away from a gang shooting even though he wants to avenge the murder of his best friend.

THE BREAKFAST CLUB

Film Data
Year: 1985
Director: John Hughes
Length: 92 minutes
Rated: R

Characters/Actors
Andrew Clark: Emilio Estevez
Richard Vernon: Paul Gleason
Brian Johnson: Anthony Michael Hall
Carl: John Kapelos
John Bender: Judd Nelson
Claire Standish: Molly Ringwald
Allison Reynolds: Ally Sheedy

Communication Courses
Group Communication
Interpersonal Communication

Communication Concepts
Critical Thinking
Group Cohesiveness
Group Development
Perception
Power
Roles
Self-Disclosure
Status

Pedagogical Perspective
The movie clearly subscribes to an "ideology of intimacy." The moral of the story appears to be that openness and honesty—even with complete strangers—will make a person happy, healthy, and wise. Something to think about as you watch the film is "Do you think the members of the Breakfast Club will remain friends?" While those who love happy endings may answer yes, many realistically acknowledge that peer pressure from the members' cliques will keep them from interacting on Monday. If this is true, then the five teenagers in the movie have handed intimate, personal, and private information to people who may be their social enemies (or at least competitors) at school. In a worst-case scenario, their self-disclosures could become inter-clique arsenal in the weeks that follow. The pros and cons of self-disclosure are an integral issue in *The Breakfast Club*.

Synopsis
The Breakfast Club takes place at an Illinois high school, where five dissimilar students are sentenced to spend a Saturday detention session together. In attendance is a "princess" (Ringwald), an "athlete" (Estevez), a "brain" (Hall), a "criminal" (Nelson), and a "basket case" (Sheedy). These titles identify the roles the students play during the school week. Because of stereotypes and status levels associated with each role, the students want nothing to do with each other at the outset of the session. However, when confronted by the authoritarian detention teacher (Gleason) and by eight hours of time to kill, the students begin to interact. Through self-disclosure they learn that they are more similar than different. Each wrestles with self-acceptance; each longs for parental approval; each

fights against peer pressure. They break through the role barriers and gain greater understanding and acceptance of each other and of themselves. They ultimately develop a group identity and dub themselves, "The Breakfast Club."

Discussion Questions

1. How do the characters deviate from their normal roles during the detention session?

2. What is the status of each character prior to the detention session? How does this change during their detention session?

3. What power resources and discussion roles are exhibited in the movie?

4. Discuss the group's developmental stages.

5. What factors contribute to the group's cohesiveness?

6. Discuss the role that perception and stereotyping play in this movie.

BREAKING AWAY

Film Data
Year: 1979
Director: Peter Yates
Length: 100 minutes
Rated: PG

Characters/Actors
Dave: Dennis Christopher
Mike: Dennis Quaid
Cyril: Daniel Stern
Moocher: Jackie Earle Haley
Dad Stoller: Paul Dooley
Mom Stoller: Barbara Barrie
Katherine: Robyn Douglass

Communication Courses
Family Communication
Group Communication
Interpersonal Communication

Communication Concepts
Leadership
Power
Relational Dialectics
Relational Stages
Self-Concept/Identity Management

Pedagogical Perspective
This film's coming-of age themes resonate with those who are trying to decide what to do about their high school friendships, relationships with their parents, and life goals. The movie's only limitations are its age (the 1979 fashions and hairstyles are dated, but the issues in the story are timeless) and its focus on male interaction. One way to address the latter issue is to compare and contrast the movie with a film that focuses on female interaction, such as *Steel Magnolias*.

Synopsis
Breaking Away is a coming-of-age film about four high school graduates from Bloomington, Indiana who are trying to figure out what to do with the rest of their lives. The young men are referred to disdainfully as "Townies" and "Cutters" by the college students at Indiana University ("Cutters" is a reference to their fathers' occupation as stone cutters in the local quarries). The group is led by Mike (Quaid), a former high school quarterback who is also the group's quarterback. Dave (Christopher) dreams of being Italian, adopting their language and bike racing as a way of escaping his lot as a Cutter. Cyril (Stern) is witty but gangly and Moocher (Haley) is shrewd but short. These odd bedfellows have agreed, according to Cyril, "to waste the rest of their lives together."
The movie is indeed about "breaking away." Dave, Moocher, and Cyril pursue jobs, girlfriends, and entrance to college—all of which threaten to break them away from the group that Mike leads with an iron fist. Dave also tries to break away from being a Cutter by pretending to be an Italian exchange student, a ruse that helps him charm an IU co-ed (Douglass). His fantasy breaks down, however, when the Italian bike team he reveres cheats its way to victory at Dave's expense. After a heart-to-heart talk with his father (Dooley), Dave decides it is okay just to be Dave Stoller—and to go to college. His new sense of identity helps him supplant Mike as leader of the group, as he

leads the Cutters to win the Little 500 bike race against the college students. The four young men, as well as Dave's parents, learn to take pride in their heritage while moving forward toward their personal goals.

Discussion Questions

1. Who is the leader of the Cutters at the beginning of the movie? Who is their leader at the end? What factors precipitate the change in leadership?

2. What resources give Mike power? How does the group counteract these resources to bring about a balance of power?

3. What relational stages and dialectics can be seen in the group's development?

4. How does Dave's self-concept develop through changes in his identity management?

BRIDGET JONES'S DIARY

Film Data
Year: 2001
Director: Sharon McGuire
Length: 98 minutes
Rated: R (language and sexuality)

Characters/Actors
Bridget Jones: Renee Zellweger
Mark Darcy: Colin Firth
Daniel Cleaver: Hugh Grant
Bridget's Mum: Gemma Jones
Bridget's Dad: Jim Broadbent
Communication Courses
Group Communication
Interpersonal Communication
Interviewing
Public Speaking

Communication Concepts
Self-Concept
Communication Competence

Pedagogical Perspective
This is a fun film that resonates with young women. Bridget's obsession with her weight, appearance, and clothing will ring true for many college-age females who are bombarded with interpersonal and media messages about thinness, beauty, and apparel. The movie also raises interesting questions about what Bridget wants in a relationship: Does she want a "good man" (Mark) or a "bad boy" (Daniel)? It appears she wants both—and the final lines of the movie suggest that Mark might be able to fill both roles. The movie is rated R for language (liberal use of the "f-word") and sexuality (including a brief nude scene).

Synopsis
Bridget Jones (Zellweger) is a single British woman in her early 30s who worries that she will die "fat and alone." By her own admission she drinks too much, smokes too much, and is overweight—all factors contributing to her fragile self-esteem. Her self-concept and communication competence (or lack thereof) are central features in her relationships with Mark Darcy (Firth) and Daniel Cleaver (Grant), both of whom vacillate between courting and dumping Bridget in a variety of romantic (and humorous) encounters. By the end of the film, Bridget decides which man truly loves her--and that she likes herself "just as she is."

Discussion Questions

1. Describe how Bridget's self-concept is constructed (and deconstructed/reconstructed) through reflected appraisal and social comparison.

2. Describe Bridget's communication competence/incompetence in interpersonal, public speaking, and interviewing situations.

CHILDREN OF A LESSER GOD

Film Data
Year: 1986
Director: Randa Haines
Length: 110 minutes
Rated: R

Characters/Actors
James Leeds: William Hurt
Sarah Norman: Marlee Matlin
Mrs. Norman: Piper Laurie
Dr. Curtis Franklin: Philip Bosco
Marian Loesser: Linda Bove

Communication Courses
Intercultural Communication
Interpersonal Communication

Communication Concepts
Communication Climate
Intercultural Communication
Power
Relational Dialectics
Relational Stages

Pedagogical Perspective
This is perhaps the richest feature film resource for the interpersonal course. In addition to the topics discussed above, the movie illustrates concepts from almost every chapter of most interpersonal communication textbooks.
The film is rated R for language and relatively discrete sex scenes. The movie is probably most appropriate for mature college students.

Synopsis
James Leeds (Hurt) is a talented and innovative teacher who accepts a new position at a school for the deaf, where he teaches students to speak. Sarah Norman (Matlin), a former student of the school, quickly captures James's attention. She is intelligent, beautiful, and feisty, yet she mops the school's floors for a living. Sarah refuses to speak or lip-read, preferring sign language and silence. James and Sarah fall into a romantic relationship that is characterized by passion and conflict. He wants to pull her into the world of speech, believing she (and he) can make more of her life if she learns to talk. She wants to pull him into the world of silence, noting that many deaf people, including her role model Marian Loesser (Bove), are quite successful without speaking. Each is proud and stubborn; each wields power in the relationship; each loves the other but wants a measure of personal and relational control. James's pressure to get Sarah to speak ultimately drives her away, but by movie's end they decide they would rather be together than apart. They agree to continue negotiating the dialectical tensions and cultural differences that mark their relationship.

Discussion Questions

1. Discuss the dialectical tension of autonomy and connection in James and Sarah's relationship.

2. Explain the climate factors that lead Sarah to feel defensive around James. How does she equalize their power imbalances?

3. Discuss how James and Sarah's relationship has dimensions of intercultural communication.

DEAD POETS SOCIETY

Film Data
Year: 1989
Director: Peter Weir
Length: 128 Minutes
Rated: PG

Characters/Actors
John Keating: Robin Williams
Neil Perry: Robert Sean Leonard
Todd Anderson: Ethan Hawke
Knox Overstreet: Josh Charles
Charlie Dalton: Gale Hansen
Richard Cameron: Dylan Kussman
Steven Meeks: Allelon Ruggiero
Gerard Pitts: James Waterston
Mr. Perry: Kurtwood Smith

Communication Courses
Group Communication
Interpersonal Communication

Communication Concepts
Communication Climate
Conflict
Critical Thinking
Defiance
Group development
Group polarization
Self-Concept

Pedagogical Perspective
Dead Poets Society is set in an all-male prep school, but the concepts of conformity, authority, and defiance are universal in their appeal and application. This entry touches on only some of the communication topics illustrated in the film. Other issues that can be analyzed include persuasion, ethics, and critical thinking. On the surface, Keating is a "good guy" who gets the students to think for themselves and to stand up for their beliefs. On the other hand, it is worth questioning whether Keating gets the students to think for themselves or whether he merely gets them to think like him. Keating's radical ideas in the hands of impressionable teenagers lead to a variety of negative outcomes, most notably Neil's suicide. Is Keating responsible, at least in part, for Neil's death? Does he appropriately mentor the students he influences? Is it ethical to encourage boys to engage in behaviors that are contrary to the wishes of their parents and the school's administration?

Synopsis
Carpe Diem: Seize the day. This is the lesson John Keating (Williams), an unorthodox teacher at an all-male prep school in New England, wants to convey to his impressionable students. Keating is an alumnus of the school, Welton Academy, and hopes to make his students as curious and iconoclastic as he was (and is). Keating encourages them to "suck the marrow out of life," pursue their dreams, and find their voice. He does so with

unusual teaching methods, such as tearing pages from textbooks, kicking soccer balls while shouting poetry, and standing on desks to gain a different perspective. These approaches are frowned upon by the administrators at conservative Welton, whose creed is "Tradition, Honor, Discipline, and Excellence."

Many of the students are captivated by Keating's ideas and ideals. At his prompting, they form a secret club called the Dead Poets Society (DPS), whose primary activity is reading poetry in a cave in the middle of the night. Many of the DPS members experiment with "risky shift" behaviors, due in part to the effect of group polarization. Charlie Dalton (Hansen), an already extroverted student, assumes a new identity as "Nuwanda" and becomes the DPS's daredevil leader. Knox Overstreet (Charles), a quiet student, chases (and ultimately catches) a football player's girlfriend. Todd Anderson (Hawke), a shy boy who is in his brother's shadow at home, gains a sense of acceptance, confidence, and self-worth. Most notably, Neil Perry (Leonard) joins a local theater production and falls in love with acting. This leads to a confrontation with his authoritarian father (Smith). When the conflict seems irresolvable, Neil commits suicide. The school fires Keating, charging that he is responsible for Neil's death because he incited the boys to rebellion. As Keating leaves the school, the boys demonstrate their loyalty to him (and defiance of the administration) by standing on their desks and calling him "Captain."

Discussion Questions

1. Discuss the group development of the Dead Poets Society (DPS).

2. What methods are used by Welton's administration to discourage defiance among the students?

3. Discuss the communication climate and conflict styles in Neil's relationship with his father (Mr. Perry).

4. How does Todd Anderson's self-concept develop over the course of the movie?

DINER

Film Data
Year: 1982
Director: Barry Levinson
Length: 110 minutes
Rated: R

Characters/Actors
Eddie: Steve Guttenberg
Shrevie: Daniel Stern
Boogie: Mickey Rourke
Fenwick: Kevin Bacon
Billy: Timothy Daly
Beth: Ellen Barkin
Carol: Kathryn Dowling
Modell: Paul Reiser

Communication Courses
Gender and Communication
Interpersonal Communication

Communication Concepts
Gender
Relational Intimacy
Self-Disclosure

Pedagogical Perspective
This is a movie that is located in both the comedy and the drama sections of video stores. On the comedy side, it has overtones of *American Graffiti* in its nostalgia and bawdy sense of humor (some of the humor may be deemed inappropriate for the classroom; teacher discretion advised). On the drama side, it has overtones of *Breaking Away* in its coming-of-age themes (in fact, Daniel Stern plays a central character in both films).

Synopsis
This is the story of a group of young men in the late 1950s who hang out with each other at a local diner. All of them have fears about growing up and relating to women. Billy (Daly) has gone away to college but returns for Eddie's (Guttenberg) wedding—and also to try to work things out with an old girlfriend (Dowling) who is pregnant with his child. Eddie is engaged but isn't quite sure why he is getting married. Shrevie (Stern) is married to Beth (Barkin), his high school sweetheart, but their relationship is rocky. Boogie (Rourke) is working his way through law school while holding down a job at a hair salon; he is also deep in debt from gambling. Fenwick (Bacon) may be the smartest of the group, but he is drowning the unhappiness of his life in booze.

The diner is the one thing that remains stable while everything else in their lives is changing. Over food, coffee, and cigarettes, they discuss the "important" matters in life such as sex, sports, and rock and roll. While their conversations may seem trivial, the time spent together cements their relationship. The guys may (and do) have troubles in their lives; they may not understand (and in fact, fear) women; they may not want to grow up; but they have each other—and the diner.

Discussion Questions

1. How do the guys in *Diner* express intimacy and friendship with each other?

2. How do the diner guys relate to the women in their lives?

ERIN BROCKOVICH

Film Data

Year: 2000
Director: Steven Soderbergh
Length: 130 minutes
Rated: R

Characters/Actors

Erin Brockovich: Julia Roberts
Ed Masry: Albert Finney
George: Aaron Eckhart
Donna Jensen: Marg Helgenberger
Pamela Duncan: Cherry Jones
Kurt Potter: Peter Coyote
Matthew: Scotty Leavenworth

Communication Courses

Interpersonal Communication
Persuasion

Communication Concepts

Communication Climate
Communication Competence
Conflict
Critical Thinking
Nonverbal (Clothing/Appearance)
Persuasion
Self-Concept

Pedagogical Perspective

This film, which is based on a true story, won an Academy Award for Julia Roberts. It is rated R because of the incessantly coarse language of the Erin Brockovich character. On the surface, this is an upbeat, "good triumphs over evil" tale in which an underdog takes on a giant utility company and justice prevails. Underneath the surface, however, is a somewhat sad story of a person with a scarred self-esteem, a fractured family life, and a lack of intimacy in most of her relationships. The movie provides a good opportunity to discuss whether Erin's ends justify her means, and whether her professional successes are worth their interpersonal costs.

Synopsis

With no money, no job, and no prospects on the horizon, Erin Brockovich (Roberts) is in a tight spot. At the end of her rope, she begs her way into a clerical position with an attorney, Ed Masry (Finney). While working there, Erin stumbles upon some medical records placed in real estate files. Confused, she questions the connection and convinces Ed to allow her to investigate. Erin ultimately discovers a Pacific Gas & Electric cover-up involving contaminated water in the local community of Hinkley, which is causing devastating illnesses among the town's residents. Although Hinkley's citizens are initially leery of taking on PG&E, Erin's persistence and concern leads them to get involved. Helping her out is her neighbor George (Eckhart), a Harley Davidson biker whose support and babysitting of Erin's children allows her the time to pursue the case. Going door to door, she signs up over 600 plantiffs, and Erin and Ed go on to win the largest settlement ever paid in a direct-action lawsuit in U.S. history: 333 million dollars.

Discussion Questions

1. Describe Erin's self-concept and sense of identity, offering examples of how she sees herself and how she portrays herself to others.

2. Describe Erin's approach to conflict management and communication climate, focusing on how she treats different people in different ways.

3. Is Erin a competent communicator? Why or why not?

THE JOY LUCK CLUB

Film Data
Year: 1993
Director: Wayne Wang
Length: 139 minutes
Rated: R

Characters/Actors
June: Ming-Na Wen
Suyuan: Kieu Chinh
Lindo: Tsai Chin
Ying Ying: France Nuyen
An-Mei: Lisa Lu
Waverly: Tamlyn Tomita
Lena: Lauren Tom
Rose: Rosalind Chao
Rich: Christopher Rich
Ted: Andrew McCarthy

Communication Courses
Family Communication
Intercultural Communication
Interpersonal Communication

Communication Concepts
Communication Climate
Conflict
Family Communication
Intercultural Communication
Self-Concept

Pedagogical Perspective
This is a gripping and complex movie that is probably best appreciated by mature college students. The film is rated R due to its intense subject matter, language, and depictions of violence and abuse (the scenes are not excessive and are pertinent to the story). The focus of the movie is mother-daughter relationships; it may thus appeal more to female students than to male students. The 139-minute running time may render it better for out-of-class viewing assignments.

Synopsis
After the death of her mother four months earlier, a young Chinese-American woman, June (Ming-Na Wen), is confronted by her mother's church friends, who call themselves The Joy Luck Club. The club consisted of June's mother, Suyuan (Kieu Chinh), and her friends Lindo (Tsia Chin), Ying Ying (France Nuyen), and An-Mei (Lisa Lu). The club informs June that her older twin sisters, who were thought to be dead, are actually alive in China. June is urged by her mother's friends to go to China to meet her sisters. The movie uses June's going-away party as a vehicle for reflecting on the struggles of the Joy Luck women and their Americanized daughters. All four came to the United States with hopes and dreams of a better life for themselves and their daughters. The mothers strive to teach their daughters values that were denied them in China: assertiveness, self-worth, and dignity for women. The lessons are hard to teach and learn, however, because of deeply rooted cultural and family patterns. The movie is a powerful statement about breaking from dysfunctional patterns while valuing culture and heritage.

Discussion Questions

1. How does culture affect the mothers' interaction with their daughters and the shaping of their self-concepts?

2. In what ways are the daughters like their mothers? (or, in the language of family systems, "In what ways are the patterns of one generation repeated by the next generation?")

3. What impact does culture have on the conflict management styles exhibited in the movie?

4. How does Waverly's boyfriend's lack of knowledge about Chinese rules lead to his intercultural incompetence at dinner?

MR. HOLLAND'S OPUS

Film Data
Year: 1996
Director: Stephen Herek
Length: 143 minutes
Rated: PG

Characters/Actors
Glenn Holland: Richard Dreyfuss
Iris Holland: Glenne Headley
Helen Jacobs: Olympia Dukakis
Cole Holland (at age 15): Joseph Anderson
Gertrude Lang: Alicia Witt
Louis Russ: Terrance Howard
Rowena Morgan: Jean Louisa Kelly

Communication Courses
Interpersonal Communication

Communication Concepts
Communication Climate
Relational Dialectics
Relational Intimacy
Self-Concept

Pedagogical Perspective
This is a heartwarming film with many lessons for interpersonal communication students. It is quite long, but there are a number of scenes throughout the film thatt show how Holland builds the self-esteem of his students and his son through confirming communication.

Synopsis
Glenn Holland (Dreyfuss) is a musician with a dream. He longs to write the symphony that plays in his head, so he takes a job as a high school music teacher to give him "free time" to compose his opus. Unexpectedly, Holland's short-term teaching job turns into a lifetime career, as he learns that investing in his students is as meaningful as investing in his music. Holland evolves from a boring teacher (and a detached father) into an inspiration for all who know him. He finishes the symphony and ultimately plays it for and with the many students whose lives he has touched over the years.

Discussion Questions

1. How do communication climates in the movie change from defensive/disconfirming to supportivc/confirming?

2. What role does Mr. Holland play in shaping the self-concepts of those who look up to him?

3. How does Mr. Holland struggle with the dialectical tension of intimacy vs. distance?

OFFICE SPACE

Film Data
Year: 1999
Director: Mike Judge
Length: 88 minutes
Rated: R

Characters/Actors
Peter Gibbons: Ron Livingston
Joanna: Jennifer Aniston
Milton: Stephen Root
Samir: Ajay Naidu
Michael Bolton: David Herman
Bill Lumbergh: Gary Cole

Communication Courses
Interpersonal Communication
Organizational Communication

Communication Concepts
Communication Climate
Classical Theory/Theory X
Conflict
Honesty/Lying
Language
Self-Concept/Identity Management

Pedagogical Perspective
The back cover of the *Office Space* video proudly announces that the film is by Mike Judge, creator of *Beavis and Butt-head*, which should serve warning that the movie has some crude content and language (as well as two brief sexual scenes). While this is a very humorous film, it touches on some serious issues that can be explored. [For example, see "Investigating the Relationship Between Superior-Subordinate Relationship Quality and Employee Dissent" by J.W. Kassing in *Communication Research Reports* (2000), Vol. 17, pp. 58-69]
One of the unstated morals of *Office Space* is that Peter's life becomes better when he stops closely managing his identity and begins doing and saying whatever he wants. While this makes for an entertaining movie (and is the premise for other entertaining films such as *Liar Liar)*, the outcomes of Peter's decisions can and should be a point of discussion for communication students. Would Peter actually be promoted to management if he ignored his boss, came to work whenever he wanted, dressed in shorts, destroyed company property, and admitted his lack of motivation to outside consultants? Probably only in Hollywood, which makes this a good case study for debating the pros and cons of identity management, honesty, and rhetorical sensitivity in the workplace.

Synopsis
Peter Gibbons (Livingston) and his colleagues Samir (Naidu) and Michael (Herman) are computer specialists who are fed up with their mundane jobs. They work at Initech Corporation, an impersonal organization with a Classical Theory/Theory X approach to management. Their boss Lumbergh (Cole) has a condescending attitude and creates a defensive communication climate with all employees, including Milton (Root), the emotionally challenged mailroom clerk who keeps threatening to "burn the building." In a hypnotherapy session, Peter loses his inhibitions and starts speaking his mind around the office. His "straight shooting" earns him a promotion while others are

downsized out of the company. Peter and his colleagues carry out a high-tech embezzling scheme to get revenge on Initech. Peter's new girlfriend Joanna (Aniston) is also fed up with her waitress job and her manager; however, she helps Peter realize that embezzling is an unethical way to handle his frustration with Initech. Ultimately, Peter and his friends move on to new horizons and Initech (quite literally) goes up in flames.

Discussion Questions

1. Describe how the Initech Corporation illustrates Classical Theory and Theory X approaches to organizational communication.

2. Describe the communication climate in manager-employee interactions in the movie.

3. What styles of conflict management are used by the managers and employees in the movie?

4. Describe the changes Peter experiences in his identity management.

SAY ANYTHING

Film Data
Year: 1989
Director: Cameron Crowe
Length: 100 minutes
Rated: PG-13

Characters/Actors
Lloyd Dobler: John Cusack
Diane Court: Ione Skye
James Court: John Mahoney
Corey Flood: Lili Taylor
D.C.: Amy Brooks
Rebecca: Pamela Segall

Communication Courses
Interpersonal Communication

Communication Concepts
Honesty/Lying
Relational Stages
Self-Disclosure

Pedagogical Perspective
This is a light, romantic comedy with a serious message about the impact of dishonesty in primary interpersonal relationships. The movie could be used in high school or college classes (Diane and Lloyd's non-depicted sexual activity might be a sensitive issue for some audiences).

Synopsis
This is a lighthearted tale about an unlikely couple. Lloyd Dobler (Cusack) is unsure what he will do after graduating from high school, except perhaps to pursue his dreams of becoming a professional kick-boxer. Diane Court (Skye) is valedictorian of her class and has plans for college—but unlike Lloyd, she has no social life. They attend a graduation party together, and Diane is pleasantly surprised at how comfortable and happy she feels around Lloyd. Their interest in each other grows and they date throughout the summer.
Diane's parents are divorced and she lives with her father (Mahoney), with whom she has always had open and honest communication. As Diane and Lloyd's relationship develops, Diane's relationship with her father begins to change. Diane's father believes Lloyd is complicating her life and he recommends that she break off her relationship with Lloyd before it becomes too serious. She acquiesces to her father's wishes. Neither Diane nor Lloyd is happy about the breakup, but she keeps telling herself it is for the best.
Diane and her father appear to have a healthy and positive relationship, but when she learns that he has engaged in illegal financial dealings involving the nursing home he runs, her trust in him is shattered. Diane realizes she wants and needs Lloyd and reaches out to him; he supports her while she deals with the devastating fact that her father is not the man she thought he was. Diane tries to reconstruct her relationship with her father before she and Lloyd fly off to England together.

Discussion Questions

1. What relational stages do Lloyd and Diane experience?

2. What were some of the reasons for self-disclosure between Diane and her father and between Lloyd and his female friends?

3. Why did Diane's father choose to lie to her about his finances? What effect did his dishonesty have on Diane and their relationship?

SWING KIDS

Film Data
Year: 1993
Director: Thomas Carter
Length: 114 minutes
Rated: PG-13

Characters/Actors
Peter: Robert Sean Leonard
Thomas: Christian Bale
Arvid: Frank Whaley
Herr Knopf: Kenneth Branagh
Evey: Tushka Bergen
Willi: David Tom
Frau Linge: Julia Stemberger
Emil: Noah Wyle
Herr Schumler: Johan Leysen

Communication Courses
Communication Theories
Persuasion

Communication Concepts
Cognitive Dissonance
Critical Thinking
Elaboration Likelihood
Social Judgment

Pedagogical Perspective
Swing Kids is an excellent tool for illustrating persuasion as a communication <u>process</u>. The characters in the movie do not experience persuasion as an immediate response to a public speech; rather, they are persuaded by a series of messages exchanged over time in interpersonal transactions. The movie also underscores the need to be critical consumers of persuasive appeals. The film has some dark moments (including one character committing suicide), but overall it is an appropriate movie for high school or college students (and it has some wonderful dance scenes to boot).

Synopsis
Swing Kids is a fictional story rooted in actual events that took place in Nazi Germany in the late 1930s. The term "Swing Kids" refers to German young people who loved American swing music and disdained the HJ (Hitler Jugend). The HJ movement was committed to nurturing young Nazis; the Swing Kids were committed to dancing and fun. The movie depicts the ongoing tension between the rebellious Swing Kids and the HJs who try to persuade them to join the Nazi cause.

At the heart of the movie is the story of three friends: Peter (Leonard), Thomas (Bale), and Arvid (Whaley). At the outset of the film, these young men are all avid fans of swing music and regularly attend underground dance sessions at local music halls. Arvid is ardently anti-Nazi, perhaps because he has the most to fear. He walks with a limp and a cane; thus, he knows he can not and will not be part of the Nazi "master race." Peter is also anti-Nazi at the beginning of the story because his father was imprisoned and died in a German jail. Thomas has the least to fear and the most to gain from the Nazis because he is looking for acceptance and status in a group. As a result, he buys into the Nazi agenda rather quickly and ends up defending it staunchly.

Swing Kids offers excellent depictions of many persuasion concepts, including fear appeals, source credibility, and

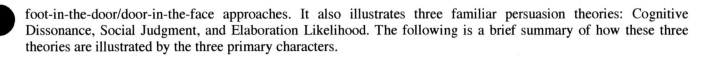

foot-in-the-door/door-in-the-face approaches. It also illustrates three familiar persuasion theories: Cognitive Dissonance, Social Judgment, and Elaboration Likelihood. The following is a brief summary of how these three theories are illustrated by the three primary characters.

Discussion Questions

   1. How is Cognitive Dissonance Theory illustrated by Arvid, Peter, and Thomas?

   2. How is Social Judgment Theory illustrated by Arvid, Peter, and Thomas?

   3. How is Elaboration Likelihood Theory illustrated by Arvid, Peter, and Thomas?

TOOTSIE

Film Data
Year: 1982
Director: Sydney Pollack
Length: 116 minutes
Rated: PG

Characters/Actors
Michael and Dorothy: Dustin Hoffman
Julie: Jessica Lange
Sandy: Teri Garr
Jeff: Bill Murray
Ron: Dabney Coleman
Les: Charles Durning
George: Sydney Pollack
John Van Horn: George Gaynes

Communication Courses
Gender and Communication
Interpersonal Communication

Communication Concepts
Conflict
Empathy
Gender
Language
Perception

Pedagogical Perspective
Tootsie is an entertaining and popular film that is familiar to many students. In the 1980s, class discussions about *Tootsie* often focused on the accuracy of stereotypes (i.e., women in the class usually argued that Ron's sexism was typical of males, while the men argued that it wasn't). Beginning in the 1990s, class discussions started revolving around issues of sexual harassment (i.e., what would happen if Ron were so blatantly sexist in today's workplace). Both topics make for engaging debates and lively discussions.

A valuable tool to enhance analysis of *Tootsie* is an interview of Dustin Hoffman by Leslie Bennetts ("Tootsie Taught Hoffman About the Sexes" was published in *The New York Times* on December 21, 1982, and is available in *The New York Times Biographical Service,* Vol. 13, No. 12, pp. 1631–32). The article describes what Hoffman learned about women and himself through playing the role of Dorothy. He says that Dorothy "made me very emotional," to the point of crying during a screen test. He claims he became "much less impatient, more tolerant of mistakes, particularly my own" as a result of the role. He also discusses prejudices about attractiveness and games between the sexes. The article is a highly recommended example of life imitating art.

Synopsis
Michael Dorsey (Hoffman) is a struggling New York actor who waits tables and teaches acting classes. He has a reputation for being difficult to work with; as a result, no one will cast him. Michael resorts to changing his identity

to a woman, Dorothy Michaels. He/she lands a part in a daytime soap opera, playing a hospital administrator who is assertive, opinionated, and feminine. Dorothy becomes a star—and a role model for women viewers around the country.

No one knows the truth except Michael's agent George (Pollack) and roommate Jeff (Murray). He hides his secret from his friend Sandy (Garr), who lost the part to Dorothy, and from fellow soap star Julie (Lange), with whom he falls in love (and whom Dorothy befriends). Director Ron (Coleman) despises Dorothy but is romantically involved with Julie. Along the way, Julie's father (Durning) falls for Dorothy, as does another soap actor (Gaynes). Thus, Michael must juggle a variety of roles and a variety of lies to maintain his job and his sanity.

The situation escalates and Michael decides he wants to just be himself again. When he reveals his identity on a live broadcast, everyone is shocked. Julie, in particular, is angry about the deception. The story ends with Michael apologizing to her, and they decide to start their relationship again as man and woman. Michael's ruse gives him a new perspective on life. He gains a sense of empathy for women and learns things about himself as a result of playing Dorothy.

Discussion Questions

1. How does playing Dorothy affect Michael's perception of male and female roles?

2. Discuss how Michael enhances his empathy and a result of playing Dorothy.

3.   How did playing the role of Dorothy change Michael's way of managing conflict?

12 ANGRY MEN

Film Data
Year: 1957
Director: Sidney Lumet
Length: 93 minutes
Rated: Not rated

Characters/Actors
Juror 1: Martin Balsam
Juror 2: John Fiedler
Juror 3: Lee Cobb
Juror 4: E. G. Marshall
Juror 5: Jack Klugman
Juror 6: Edward Binns
Juror 7: Jack Warden
Juror 8: Henry Fonda
Juror 9: Joseph Sweeney
Juror 10: Ed Begley
Juror 11: George Voskovec
Juror 12: Robert Webber

Communication Courses
Interpersonal Communication
Group Communication
Listening
Persuasion

Communication Concepts
Communication Climate
Conformity
Critical Thinking
Defiance
Group Roles
Listening
Perception
Persuasion
Power

Pedagogical Perspective
This movie is a black-and-white "golden oldie" that still captures contemporary audiences. The jurors are an all-white, all-male group, leading to possible limitations in applications to diverse student populations (this could be a point for discussion). The notion raised in Question 2—that Fonda is not impartial and uses questionable tactics to achieve his goals—is not popular with some who prefer to view Fonda as a hero. An interesting way to view the film is to watch it (perhaps a second viewing) pretending to know for a fact that the defendant did indeed murder his father. From this perspective, Fonda is using his formidable persuasive powers to free a guilty man. Thus, the same behaviors that would normally be seen as heroic are now perceived as villainous by those who have been primed to view Fonda critically. The goal of this exercise is neither to impugn nor vindicate Fonda; rather, the goal is to help us see that (a) communication techniques can be used for positive or negative outcomes, (b) perception is

influenced by assumptions, (c) even heroes and happy endings need to be critically evaluated (see also *Dead Poets Society, Erin Brockovich, The Breakfast Club*).

Synopsis

Twelve nameless strangers stuck together in a hot New York courtroom must determine the fate of an 18-year-old defendant accused of murdering his father. If they find the young man guilty, there is a mandatory death sentence. It appears to be an open-and-shut case, and eleven of the twelve jurors vote guilty on the first ballot. The one who votes not guilty (Fonda) does so because he won't send the defendant to death without "at least talking about it." As a result, they become twelve angry men, arguing for hours about the verdict.

The wide range of the jurors' personalities and backgrounds make the deliberations both difficult and intriguing. Juror 1 (Balsam) is a high-school football coach who, as foreman of the jury, wants a minimum of conflict and a maximum of structure (he gets neither). Juror 8 (Fonda), struggling with ethical issues of reasonable doubt, persuades the jurors to closely examine the evidence and their personal biases. Fonda's primary adversary is Juror 3 (Cobb), an angry father who, because of his poor relationship with his son, categorizes the defendant as a rebellious kid and wants to persecute him. Similar to Cobb, Juror 10 (Begley) is a sour and prejudicial man who stereotypes the defendant as slum "trash" and a "born liar." Juror 5 (Klugman), a streetwise man from the poor side of town, challenges the prejudices of Cobb and Begley and provides valuable information about the murder weapon. A foreign-born watchmaker, Juror 11 (Voskovec) focuses the jury on the beauty and responsibility of the American judicial process. He argues with baseball-loving Juror 7 (Warden), who conforms with the majority in order to quickly end the deliberations so he can attend a ballgame. Juror 2 (Fiedler) is a timid, unassuming bank clerk and Juror 9 (Sweeney) is an old man who struggles to be heard; both are befriended and empowered by Fonda. Juror 12 (Webber) continually strays off course with advertising stories and slogans; Juror 6 (Binns) is a blue-collar worker who is somewhat intimidated by the proceedings. Finally, Juror 4 (Marshall) is a serious, logical stockbroker who refuses to budge until he is presented with sound reasons for changing his mind. (Note: For ease of reading, actors' names will be used rather than juror numbers)

One by one, Fonda convinces the jurors that there is reasonable doubt about the defendant's guilt. The tide of conformity that works against him at the outset of the story works for him by story's end. Hidden prejudices are brought into the open, specious evidence is questioned, and faulty logic is (for the most part) challenged. The defendant is declared not guilty and the jurors walk away richer for the process.

Discussion Questions

1. What communication techniques does Fonda use to change the jurors' minds and votes?

2. Is Fonda impartial about the verdict? If not, what methods does he use to pursue his agenda?

3. What conformity pressures and defiance-extinguishing strategies are used in the jury's decision-making processes?

4. Discuss leadership behaviors and power resources within the jury.

WHEN HARRY MET SALLY...

Film Data
Year: 1989
Director: Rob Reiner
Length: 96 minutes
Rated: R

Characters/Actors
Harry Burns: Billy Crystal
Sally Albright: Meg Ryan
Marie: Carrie Fisher
Jess: Bruno Kirby
Communication Courses
Gender and Communication
Interpersonal Communication

Communication Concepts
Gender
Relational Stages

Pedagogical Perspective

This is a sweet, funny, and perceptive film that is well known to (and loved by) most college students. The now-famous "orgasm scene" and occasional rough language may make viewing uncomfortable for some, but most are familiar enough with the film that it doesn't faze them. This film is an ideal way to study relational stages. More information about gender issues in the film can be found in Em Griffin's textbook, *A First Look at Communication Theory*. *When Harry Met Sally* is also a useful tool for discussing topics such as communication climate (which slowly changes from chilly to warm), conflict, and perception.

Synopsis

Harry Burns (Crystal) and Sally Albright (Ryan) are virtual strangers who get together for purely functional reasons: A cross-country car ride in which they share gas costs and driving. She quickly sizes him up as crude and insensitive; he appraises her as naive and obsessive. By the time they finish their journey, they are glad to part ways. However, they continue bumping into each other in the years that follow. Slowly but surely, a friendship develops between them—something that Harry declared could never happen because "men and women can't be friends; the sex thing always gets in the way." Harry and Sally try to set each other up with their friends Jess (Kirby) and Marie (Fisher), but Jess and Marie fall for each other instead. Harry and Sally try dating other people, but clearly they care deeply for each other. Ultimately, their friendship turns into love—but not without some sharp disagreements (and a short breakup) over the role that sex plays in male–female relationships. Their breakup ends when they realize how much they both like and love each other. They marry and (presumably) live happily ever after.

Discussion Questions

1. What gender differences are evident in Harry and Sally's communication?

2. How does (or doesn't) Harry and Sally's relationship match Knapp's model of relational stages?

YOU'VE GOT MAIL

Film Data
Year: 1998
Director: Nora Ephron
Length: 120 minutes
Rated: PG

Characters/Actors
Kathleen Kelly: Meg Ryan
Joe Fox: Tom Hanks
Patricia Eden: Parker Posey
Frank Navasky: Greg Kinnear
Christina: Heather Burns
George Pappas: Steve Zahn
Birdie: Jean Stapleton

Communication Courses
Gender and Communication
Interpersonal Communication

Communication Concepts
Communication Climate
Communication Competence
Computer-Mediated Communication
Gender
Identity/Impression Management
Relational Intimacy
Self-Disclosure

Pedagogical Perspective
This is a lightweight romantic comedy, whose greatest instructional value is that it illustrates the role of computer-mediated communication in building and maintaining interpersonal relationships. CMC is likely to be a hot topic in communication courses for years to come. A good upper-level reading to accompany this movie is J.B. Walther's "Computer-Mediated Communication: Impersonal, Interpersonal, and Hyperpersonal Interaction" in *Communication Research*, Vol. 23, pp. 3-43.

Synopsis
Joe Fox (Hanks) and Kathleen Kelly (Ryan) are thirty-something New Yorkers who detest each other—or at least they think they do. Face-to-face, Kathleen despises Joe because his discount bookstore chain threatens to bankrupt Kathleen's family-owned bookshop. She also hates Joe's arrogant, self-absorbed style of communicating. In cyberspace, however, Joe seems like a different person. Unbeknownst to both Joe and Kathleen, they have been communicating with each other anonymously for months after meeting in an online chat room, using the names "NY152" and "Shopgirl." The e-mail messages Joe sends Kathleen are tender and self-disclosing. She falls for NY152 without knowing that the enchanting messages are written by the same man she can't stand in person. Joe learns of Kathleen's cyber-identity before she learns of his, and he slowly realizes the need to change his face-to-face presentational style. He begins revealing his softer side in their in-person encounters. In true Hollywood fashion, Kathleen and Joe ultimately find love in person—and presumably live happily ever after.

Discussion Questions

1. Describe the communication climate between Kathleen and Joe in their face-to-face communication. What factors are involved in creating this climate?

2. Describe the communication climate between Kathleen and Joe in their online, computer-mediated communication (CMC). What factors are involved in creating this climate?

3. How do Kathleen and Joe transform their face-to-face relationship from negative to positive?

SECTION III

FEATURE FILM WEB SITES OF INTEREST:

Film Clips Online
Filmclipsonline.com

Teach With Movies
teachwithmovies.org

Hartwick Classic Film Leadership Cases
http://www.hartwickinstitute.org/Store.aspx?Action=Sort&Type=Film

The Internet Movie Database
imdb.com

Film.Com
film.com

Movie Review Query Engine
mrqe.com

Roger Ebert Print Reviews
suntimes.com/ebert/index.html